IN SPIRIT & IN TRUTH

A STUDY OF BIBLICAL WORSHIP

SHE READS TRUTH

I knew right then that
I was His, *and my heart
responded in kind.*

THIS BOOK BELONGS TO

_____

START DATE

_____

SHE READS TRUTH

EXECUTIVE

FOUNDER/CHIEF EXECUTIVE OFFICER
Raechel Myers

CO-FOUNDER/CHIEF CONTENT OFFICER
Amanda Bible Williams

**CHIEF OPERATING OFFICER/
CREATIVE DIRECTOR**
Ryan Myers

EXECUTIVE ASSISTANT
Catherine Cromer

EDITORIAL

CONTENT DIRECTOR
John Greco, MDiv

MANAGING EDITOR
Jessica Lamb

KIDS READ TRUTH EDITOR
Melanie Rainer, MATS

CONTENT EDITOR
Kara Gause

EDITORIAL ASSISTANT
Ellen Taylor

MARKETING

MARKETING MANAGER
Kayla Stinson

SOCIAL MEDIA STRATEGIST
Ansley Rushing

COMMUNITY SUPPORT SPECIALIST
Margot Williams

CREATIVE

LEAD DESIGNER
Kelsea Allen

ARTIST IN RESIDENCE
Emily Knapp

DESIGNERS
Abbey Benson
Davis DeLisi

SHIPPING & LOGISTICS

LOGISTICS MANAGER
Lauren Gloyne

SHIPPING MANAGER
Sydney Bess

FULFILLMENT COORDINATOR
Katy McKnight

FULFILLMENT SPECIALISTS
Sam Campos
Julia Rogers

SUBSCRIPTION INQUIRIES
orders@shereadstruth.com

CONTRIBUTORS

COVER PHOTOGRAPHER
Abigail Laliberte

PHOTOGRAPHERS
Abigail Laliberte (12, 14, 20,
34, 40, 50, 60, 66)
Erin Krespan (14, 86)
Natalie Gettis (80)

@SHEREADSTRUTH

Download the
She Reads Truth app,
available for iOS
and Android.

SHEREADSTRUTH.COM

SHE READS TRUTH™

© 2019 by She Reads Truth, LLC

All rights reserved.

All photography used by permission.

ISBN 978-1-949526-40-0

All Scripture is taken from the Christian Standard Bible®. Copyright © 2017 by Holman Bible Publishers. Used by permission. Christian Standard Bible® and CSB® are federally registered trademarks of Holman Bible Publishers.

Research support provided by Logos Bible Software™. Learn more at logos.com.

This book was printed offset in Nashville, Tennessee, on 70# Lynx Opaque. Cover is 100# Cougar Opaque with a soft touch lamination.

Amanda

Amanda Bible Williams
CO-FOUNDER & CHIEF
CONTENT OFFICER

I was five years old, standing with my mom and brother in a pew near the front of the sanctuary. We were singing a hymn and I had my eyes closed, my hands held in front of me with my palms facing up as if carrying an invisible tray. This is my earliest memory of worship.

I didn't know to call it that. I was just responding to the reality of who God showed Himself to be. Somehow—maybe through the Scripture read from the pulpit or a truth proclaimed in that hymn, or maybe through whispers from the Holy Spirit to my heart—I caught a glimpse of God, big and strong and holy, but also good and loving. I felt connected to Him, like I knew Him and He knew me. It didn't matter that I was small; I knew right then that I was His, and my heart responded in kind.

That moment in my memory marks the beginning of a lifelong journey of worship, of learning to respond to God with all of myself. There are times this resembles that day in the church pew, my heart swelling in worship as the pipe organ plays and the congregation sings. More often it takes a subtler form, a different shape of surrender for each circumstance and season. Sometimes my worship is misplaced; like a train without tracks, I give my awe and reverence to something other than my Creator.

If worship is more than singing on Sunday morning, what is it? Jesus told the Samaritan woman at the well that true worshipers worship "in Spirit and in truth" (Jn 4:23). How do we worship with a heart tuned to the Spirit of the Lord and tethered to the truth of His Word?

These are the questions this book explores. Each day we will read about an aspect of worship from Scripture, spending time reflecting on what it looks like in our lives. While these two weeks will not give us an exhaustive look at the topic of worship in the Bible, our prayer is that we'll walk away with a fuller understanding of what "worship in spirit and in truth" means for us and the God who made us.

Be sure not to miss the extras on corporate worship and false worship on pages 72 and 41, both so helpful in forming a biblical framework for worship. And make use of the ample journaling space provided throughout! This study proved to be an introspective one for our team, so we've allowed plenty of room for personal reflection.

Like that little girl with hands stretched out, I am still learning how to worship. Join me as we learn together, and may our lives reflect more of God's goodness and glory as a result.

Worship, at its core, is a joyful act. The vibrant "tennis ball" green used sparingly throughout the book brings focus and movement to the moody images and muted layouts.

Reflect & Pray

Reflect & Pray

Reflect & Pray

The quiet moments in the book's design evoke the reverence and awe inherent to biblical worship, inviting the reader to rest and reflect.

High-contrast lifestyle photography was used throughout the book as a reminder that worship connects imperfect humanity with a holy God and happens in everyday spaces.

She Reads Truth is a community of women dedicated to reading the Word of God every day.

The Bible is living and active, breathed out by God, and we confidently hold it higher than anything we can do or say. This book focuses primarily on Scripture, with bonus resources to facilitate deeper engagement with God's Word.

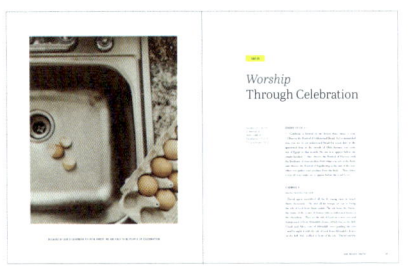

SCRIPTURE READING

Designed for a Monday start, this Study Book presents daily readings on the topic of biblical worship.

RESPONSE

Each daily reading closes with questions for reflection and space for journaling and prayer.

GRACE DAY

Use Saturdays to pray, rest, and reflect on what you've read.

WEEKLY TRUTH

Sundays are set aside for weekly Scripture memorization.

Find the corresponding memory cards in the back of this book.

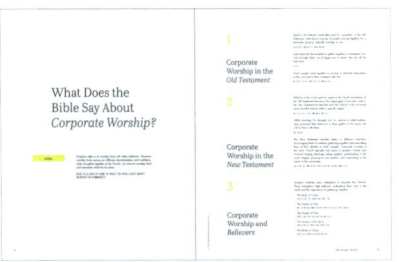

EXTRAS

This book features additional tools to help you gain a deeper understanding of the text.

In Spirit & in Truth: A Study of Biblical Worship

2 Weeks

PLAN OVERVIEW

Worship is our response to the presence and character of God. It is a way of life—spontaneous action and worthwhile discipline. It is also a gift, and we are both givers and recipients, for worship allows us the incredible privilege of drawing near to our Creator. As God's people, everything we do can and should be worship. In this two-week study, we...

For added community and conversation, join us in the **In Spirit & in Truth: A Study of Biblical Worship** reading plan on the She Reads Truth app or at SheReadsTruth.com.

Table of
Contents

We are called to an *everlasting preoccupation* with God.

A.W. TOZER

WORSHIP IS OUR RESPONSE TO WHO GOD IS AND WHAT HE HAS DONE.

What Is Worship?

DEUTERONOMY 6:13-14

13 Fear the LORD your God, worship him, and take your oaths in his name. 14 Do not follow other gods, the gods of the peoples around you...

ISAIAH 40:18-31

18 With whom will you compare God?
What likeness will you set up for comparison with him?
19 An idol?—something that a smelter casts
and a metalworker plates with gold
and makes silver chains for?
20 A poor person contributes wood for a pedestal
that will not rot.
He looks for a skilled craftsman
to set up an idol that will not fall over.

21 Do you not know?
Have you not heard?
Has it not been declared to you
from the beginning?
Have you not considered
the foundations of the earth?

> *"To whom will you compare me, or who is my equal?" asks the Holy One.*
>
> ISAIAH 40:25

²² God is enthroned above the circle of the earth;
its inhabitants are like grasshoppers.
He stretches out the heavens like thin cloth
and spreads them out like a tent to live in.
²³ He reduces princes to nothing
and makes judges of the earth like a wasteland.
²⁴ They are barely planted, barely sown,
their stem hardly takes root in the ground
when he blows on them and they wither,
and a whirlwind carries them away like stubble.

²⁵ "To whom will you compare me,
or who is my equal?" asks the Holy One.
²⁶ Look up and see!
Who created these?
He brings out the stars by number;
he calls all of them by name.
Because of his great power and strength,
not one of them is missing.

²⁷ Jacob, why do you say,
and, Israel, why do you assert:
"My way is hidden from the LORD,
and my claim is ignored by my God"?

²⁸ Do you not know?
Have you not heard?
The LORD is the everlasting God,
the Creator of the whole earth.
He never becomes faint or weary;
there is no limit to his understanding.
²⁹ He gives strength to the faint
and strengthens the powerless.
³⁰ Youths may become faint and weary,
and young men stumble and fall,
³¹ but those who trust in the LORD
will renew their strength;
they will soar on wings like eagles;
they will run and not become weary,
they will walk and not faint.

MATTHEW 14:22-33

WALKING ON THE WATER

²² Immediately he made the disciples get into the boat and go ahead of him to the other side, while he dismissed the crowds. ²³ After dismissing the crowds, he went up on the mountain by himself to pray. Well into the night, he was

there alone. [24] Meanwhile, the boat was already some distance from land, battered by the waves, because the wind was against them. [25] Jesus came toward them walking on the sea very early in the morning. [26] When the disciples saw him walking on the sea, they were terrified. "It's a ghost!" they said, and they cried out in fear.

[27] Immediately Jesus spoke to them. "Have courage! It is I. Don't be afraid."

[28] "Lord, if it's you," Peter answered him, "command me to come to you on the water."

[29] He said, "Come."

And climbing out of the boat, Peter started walking on the water and came toward Jesus. [30] But when he saw the strength of the wind, he was afraid, and beginning to sink he cried out, "Lord, save me!"

[31] Immediately Jesus reached out his hand, caught hold of him, and said to him, "You of little faith, why did you doubt?"

[32] When they got into the boat, the wind ceased. [33] Then those in the boat worshiped him and said, "Truly you are the Son of God."

JOSHUA 24:14–15

THE COVENANT RENEWAL

[14] Therefore, fear the LORD and worship him in sincerity and truth. Get rid of the gods your fathers worshiped beyond the Euphrates River and in Egypt, and worship the LORD. [15] But if it doesn't please you to worship the LORD, choose for yourselves today: Which will you worship—the gods your fathers worshiped beyond the Euphrates River or the gods of the Amorites in whose land you are living? As for me and my family, we will worship the LORD.

JOHN 4:21–24

[21] Jesus told her, "Believe me, woman, an hour is coming when you will worship the Father neither on this mountain nor in Jerusalem. [22] You Samaritans worship what you do not know. We worship what we do know, because salvation is from the Jews. [23] But an hour is coming, and is now here, when the true worshipers will worship the Father in Spirit and in truth. Yes, the Father wants such people to worship him. [24] God is spirit, and those who worship him must worship in Spirit and in truth."

Reflect & Pray

DAY 1

How do you define worship?

What do these scriptures say about worship?

WE CAN PRAISE GOD THROUGH MUSIC IN TIMES OF JOY AND SORROW.

Worship Through Song

PSALM 33:1-9

PRAISE TO THE CREATOR

[1] Rejoice in the LORD, you righteous ones;
praise from the upright is beautiful.
[2] Praise the LORD with the lyre;
make music to him with a ten-stringed harp.
[3] Sing a new song to him;
play skillfully on the strings, with a joyful shout.

[4] For the word of the LORD is right,
and all his work is trustworthy.
[5] He loves righteousness and justice;
the earth is full of the LORD's unfailing love.

[6] The heavens were made by the word of the LORD,
and all the stars, by the breath of his mouth.
[7] He gathers the water of the sea into a heap;
he puts the depths into storehouses.
[8] Let the whole earth fear the LORD;
let all the inhabitants of the world stand in awe of him.
[9] For he spoke, and it came into being;
he commanded, and it came into existence.

About midnight Paul and Silas were praying and singing hymns to God, and the prisoners were listening to them.

ACTS 16:25

PSALM 147:1-9

GOD RESTORES JERUSALEM

[1] Hallelujah!
How good it is to sing to our God,
for praise is pleasant and lovely.

[2] The LORD rebuilds Jerusalem;
he gathers Israel's exiled people.
[3] He heals the brokenhearted
and bandages their wounds.
[4] He counts the number of the stars;
he gives names to all of them.
[5] Our Lord is great, vast in power;
his understanding is infinite.
[6] The LORD helps the oppressed
but brings the wicked to the ground.

[7] Sing to the LORD with thanksgiving;
play the lyre to our God,
[8] who covers the sky with clouds,
prepares rain for the earth,
and causes grass to grow on the hills.
[9] He provides the animals with their food,
and the young ravens, what they cry for.

EXODUS 15:19-21

[19] When Pharaoh's horses with his chariots and horsemen went into the sea, the LORD brought the water of the sea back over them. But the Israelites walked through the sea on dry ground. [20] Then the prophetess Miriam, Aaron's sister, took a tambourine in her hand, and all the women came out following her with tambourines and dancing. [21] Miriam sang to them:

Sing to the LORD,
for he is highly exalted;
he has thrown the horse
and its rider into the sea.

ACTS 16:16-34

PAUL AND SILAS IN PRISON

[16] Once, as we were on our way to prayer, a slave girl met us who had a spirit by which she predicted the future. She made a large profit for her owners by fortune-telling. [17] As she followed Paul and us she cried out, "These men, who are proclaiming to you the way of salvation, are the servants of the Most High God." [18] She did this for many days.

Paul was greatly annoyed. Turning to the spirit, he said, "I command you in the name of Jesus Christ to come out of her!" And it came out right away.

[19] When her owners realized that their hope of profit was gone, they seized Paul and Silas and dragged them into the marketplace to the authorities. [20] Bringing them before the chief magistrates, they said, "These men are seriously disturbing our city. They are Jews [21] and are promoting customs that are not legal for us as Romans to adopt or practice." [22] The crowd joined in the attack against them, and the chief magistrates stripped off their clothes and ordered them to be beaten with rods. [23] After they had severely flogged them, they threw them in jail, ordering the jailer to guard them carefully. [24] Receiving such an order, he put them into the inner prison and secured their feet in the stocks.

A MIDNIGHT DELIVERANCE

[25] About midnight Paul and Silas were praying and singing hymns to God, and the prisoners were listening to them. [26] Suddenly there was such a violent earthquake that the foundations of the jail were shaken, and immediately all the doors were opened, and everyone's chains came loose. [27] When the jailer woke up and saw the doors of the prison standing open, he drew his sword and was going to kill himself, since he thought the prisoners had escaped.

[28] But Paul called out in a loud voice, "Don't harm yourself, because we're all here!"

[29] The jailer called for lights, rushed in, and fell down trembling before Paul and Silas. [30] He escorted them out and said, "Sirs, what must I do to be saved?"

[31] They said, "Believe in the Lord Jesus, and you will be saved—you and your household." [32] And they spoke the word of the Lord to him along with everyone in his house. [33] He took them the same hour of the night and washed their wounds. Right away he and all his family were baptized. [34] He brought them into his house, set a meal before them, and rejoiced because he had come to believe in God with his entire household.

COLOSSIANS 3:16

Let the word of Christ dwell richly among you, in all wisdom teaching and admonishing one another through psalms, hymns, and spiritual songs, singing to God with gratitude in your hearts.

Reflect & Pray

What do these scriptures say about worship through song?

What does worship through song look like in this season of your life?

All Creatures of *Our God and King*

TEXT	TRANSLATED	TUNE	ARRANGED
St. Francis of Assisi	William H. Draper	Geistliche Kirchengesänge	Ralph Vaughan Williams
1225	1919	1623	1906

LIFT UP YOUR VOICE AND WITH US SING <mark>ALLELUIA, ALLELUIA!</mark>

WE WORSHIP GOD THROUGH SERVICE TO HIM AND OTHERS BECAUSE OF WHO HE IS.

Worship Through Service

Matthew 25:31–46
Isaiah 58:6–11
Mark 10:35–45

MATTHEW 25:31–46

THE SHEEP AND THE GOATS

31 "When the Son of Man comes in his glory, and all the angels with him, then he will sit on his glorious throne. 32 All the nations will be gathered before him, and he will separate them one from another, just as a shepherd separates the sheep from the goats. 33 He will put the sheep on his right and the goats on the left. 34 Then the King will say to those on his right, 'Come, you who are blessed by my Father; inherit the kingdom prepared for you from the foundation of the world.

35 "'For I was hungry and you gave me something to eat; I was thirsty and you gave me something to drink; I was a stranger and you took me in; 36 I was naked and you clothed me; I was sick and you took care of me; I was in prison and you visited me.'

37 "Then the righteous will answer him, 'Lord, when did we see you hungry and feed you, or thirsty and give you something to drink? 38 When did we see you a stranger and take you in, or without clothes and clothe you? 39 When did we see you sick, or in prison, and visit you?'

> "For even the Son of Man did not come to be served, but to serve, and *to give his life as a ransom for many.*"

MARK 10:45

40 "And the King will answer them, 'Truly I tell you, whatever you did for one of the least of these brothers and sisters of mine, you did for me.'

41 "Then he will also say to those on the left, 'Depart from me, you who are cursed, into the eternal fire prepared for the devil and his angels! 42 For I was hungry and you gave me nothing to eat; I was thirsty and you gave me nothing to drink; 43 I was a stranger and you didn't take me in; I was naked and you didn't clothe me, sick and in prison and you didn't take care of me.'

44 "Then they too will answer, 'Lord, when did we see you hungry, or thirsty, or a stranger, or without clothes, or sick, or in prison, and not help you?'

45 "Then he will answer them, 'Truly I tell you, whatever you did not do for one of the least of these, you did not do for me.'

46 "And they will go away into eternal punishment, but the righteous into eternal life."

ISAIAH 58:6-11

6 "Isn't this the fast I choose:
To break the chains of wickedness,
to untie the ropes of the yoke,
to set the oppressed free,
and to tear off every yoke?
7 Is it not to share your bread with the hungry,
to bring the poor and homeless into your house,
to clothe the naked when you see him,
and not to ignore your own flesh and blood?
8 Then your light will appear like the dawn,
and your recovery will come quickly.
Your righteousness will go before you,
and the Lord's glory will be your rear guard.

9 At that time, when you call, the Lord will answer;
when you cry out, he will say, 'Here I am.'
If you get rid of the yoke among you,
the finger-pointing and malicious speaking,
10 and if you offer yourself to the hungry,
and satisfy the afflicted one,
then your light will shine in the darkness,
and your night will be like noonday.

[11] The LORD will always lead you,
satisfy you in a parched land,
and strengthen your bones.
You will be like a watered garden
and like a spring whose water never runs dry."

MARK 10:35-45

SUFFERING AND SERVICE

[35] James and John, the sons of Zebedee, approached him and said, "Teacher, we want you to do whatever we ask you."

[36] "What do you want me to do for you?" he asked them.

[37] They answered him, "Allow us to sit at your right and at your left in your glory."

[38] Jesus said to them, "You don't know what you're asking. Are you able to drink the cup I drink or to be baptized with the baptism I am baptized with?"

[39] "We are able," they told him.

Jesus said to them, "You will drink the cup I drink, and you will be baptized with the baptism I am baptized with. [40] But to sit at my right or left is not mine to give; instead, it is for those for whom it has been prepared."

[41] When the ten disciples heard this, they began to be indignant with James and John. [42] Jesus called them over and said to them, "You know that those who are regarded as rulers of the Gentiles lord it over them, and those in high positions act as tyrants over them. [43] But it is not so among you. On the contrary, whoever wants to become great among you will be your servant, [44] and whoever wants to be first among you will be a slave to all. [45] For even the Son of Man did not come to be served, but to serve, and to give his life as a ransom for many."

Reflect & Pray

DAY 3

What do these scriptures say about worship through service?

What does service look like in this season of your life?

WE WORSHIP GOD BY OBEYING HIS WORD.

Worship Through Obedience

Daniel 6:1–24
Colossians 3:17
Psalm 19:7–14
Micah 6:8

DANIEL 6:1-24

THE PLOT AGAINST DANIEL

[1] Darius decided to appoint 120 satraps over the kingdom, stationed throughout the realm, [2] and over them three administrators, including Daniel. These satraps would be accountable to them so that the king would not be defrauded. [3] Daniel distinguished himself above the administrators and satraps because he had an extraordinary spirit, so the king planned to set him over the whole realm. [4] The administrators and satraps, therefore, kept trying to find a charge against Daniel regarding the kingdom. But they could find no charge or corruption, for he was trustworthy, and no negligence or corruption was found in him. [5] Then these men said, "We will never find any charge against this Daniel unless we find something against him concerning the law of his God."

[6] So the administrators and satraps went together to the king and said to him, "May King Darius live forever. [7] All the administrators of the kingdom, the prefects, satraps, advisers, and governors have agreed that the king should establish an ordinance and enforce an edict that for thirty days, anyone who petitions any god or man except you, the king, will be thrown into the lions' den. [8] Therefore, Your Majesty, establish the edict and sign the document so that, as

> *The command of the LORD is radiant, making the eyes light up.*
>
> PSALM 19:8

a law of the Medes and Persians, it is irrevocable and cannot be changed." ⁹ So King Darius signed the written edict.

DANIEL IN THE LIONS' DEN

¹⁰ When Daniel learned that the document had been signed, he went into his house. The windows in its upstairs room opened toward Jerusalem, and three times a day he got down on his knees, prayed, and gave thanks to his God, just as he had done before. ¹¹ Then these men went as a group and found Daniel petitioning and imploring his God. ¹² So they approached the king and asked about his edict: "Didn't you sign an edict that for thirty days any person who petitions any god or man except you, the king, will be thrown into the lions' den?"

The king answered, "As a law of the Medes and Persians, the order stands and is irrevocable."

¹³ Then they replied to the king, "Daniel, one of the Judean exiles, has ignored you, the king, and the edict you signed, for he prays three times a day." ¹⁴ As soon as the king heard this, he was very displeased; he set his mind on rescuing Daniel and made every effort until sundown to deliver him.

¹⁵ Then these men went together to the king and said to him, "You know, Your Majesty, that it is a law of the Medes and Persians that no edict or ordinance the king establishes can be changed."

¹⁶ So the king gave the order, and they brought Daniel and threw him into the lions' den. The king said to Daniel, "May your God, whom you continually serve, rescue you!" ¹⁷ A stone was brought and placed over the mouth of the den. The king sealed it with his own signet ring and with the signet rings of his nobles, so that nothing in regard to Daniel could be changed. ¹⁸ Then the king went to his palace and spent the night fasting. No diversions were brought to him, and he could not sleep.

DANIEL RELEASED

¹⁹ At the first light of dawn the king got up and hurried to the lions' den. ²⁰ When he reached the den, he cried out in anguish to Daniel. "Daniel, servant of the living God," the king said, "has your God, whom you continually serve, been able to rescue you from the lions?"

²¹ Then Daniel spoke with the king: "May the king live forever. ²² My God sent his angel and shut the lions' mouths; and they haven't harmed me, for I was found innocent before him. And also before you, Your Majesty, I have not done harm."

²³ The king was overjoyed and gave orders to take Daniel out of the den. When Daniel was brought up from the den, he was found to be unharmed, for he trusted in his God. ²⁴ The king then gave the command, and those men who had maliciously accused Daniel were brought and thrown into the lions' den—they, their children, and their wives. They had not reached the bottom of the den before the lions overpowered them and crushed all their bones.

COLOSSIANS 3:17

And whatever you do, in word or in deed, do everything in the name of the Lord Jesus, giving thanks to God the Father through him.

PSALM 19:7-14

[7] The instruction of the LORD is perfect,
renewing one's life;
the testimony of the LORD is trustworthy,
making the inexperienced wise.
[8] The precepts of the LORD are right,
making the heart glad;
the command of the LORD is radiant,
making the eyes light up.
[9] The fear of the LORD is pure,
enduring forever;
the ordinances of the LORD are reliable
and altogether righteous.
[10] They are more desirable than gold—
than an abundance of pure gold;
and sweeter than honey
dripping from a honeycomb.
[11] In addition, your servant is warned by them,
and in keeping them there is an abundant reward.

[12] Who perceives his unintentional sins?
Cleanse me from my hidden faults.
[13] Moreover, keep your servant from willful sins;
do not let them rule me.
Then I will be blameless
and cleansed from blatant rebellion.
[14] May the words of my mouth
and the meditation of my heart
be acceptable to you,
LORD, my rock and my Redeemer.

MICAH 6:8

Mankind, he has told each of you what is good
and what it is the LORD requires of you:
to act justly,
to love faithfulness,
and to walk humbly with your God.

Reflect & Pray

DAY 4

What do these scriptures say about worship through obedience?

What does obedience look like in this season of your life?

IN SPIRIT & IN TRUTH: A STUDY OF BIBLICAL WORSHIP

False Worship

False Worship

EXTRA

As God's image-bearers, it is our privilege and purpose to worship our Creator. Though it's what we were made to do, we sometimes get it wrong.

FOLLOWING ARE SOME OF THE MANY EXAMPLES OF FALSE WORSHIP FOUND IN THE BIBLE.

Idolatrous Worship

ONE

We are never to worship created things, but God and God alone.

While waiting for Moses to return from atop Mount Sinai, the Israelites grew impatient and demanded that Aaron make gods for them to worship. So Aaron made a golden calf, and the people offered sacrifices to it. Their actions were a direct violation of the commandment, "Do not make an idol for yourself" (Ex 20:4).

EX 32

Disobedient Worship

TWO

Worship cannot come from an act of disobedience.

Saul, the first king of Israel, had been told to wait for the prophet Samuel at Gilgal before proceeding into battle against the Philistines. When seven days had passed, Saul decided to take matters into his own hands and offered a burnt offering to the Lord. But he was not a priest, and his offering was a violation of God's specific command to wait. As a consequence, God took away Saul's kingdom.

1SM 13:1–15

Irreverent Worship

THREE

We must never forget the holiness of God.

The ark of the covenant was placed on a cart in order to transport it to Jerusalem, where it was to reside permanently. The people walking with the ark worshiped God with music and dancing as they went. Along the way, the oxen pulling the cart stumbled, and a man named Uzzah reached out to steady the ark. "God struck him dead on the spot for his irreverence" (2Sm 6:7). Though we may feel for Uzzah, as David did (v. 8), the Lord had commanded that no one touch the ark (Nm 4:15). Today, we are invited to come boldly before God's throne (Heb 4:16), but we must never forget that the Lord is holy, deserving all our reverence and respect.

2SM 6:1–11

Worship Without Cost

FOUR

Worship should require something from us.

David wanted to make an offering to the Lord at Araunah the Jebusite's threshing floor, the future site of the temple in Jerusalem. Araunah offered to give David the land and whatever oxen or wood his sacrifice required without charge, but David wisely refused, saying, "I will not offer to the LORD my God burnt offerings that cost me nothing" (2Sm 24:24). An act of worship is our offering to God, but it must be our offering to make.

2SM 24:18–25

Worship of Other Gods

FIVE

We are to give our worship to God Most High and to no other gods.

Throughout Israel's history, the people turned to false gods, often combining their worship of the one true God with pagan practices and always violating the commandment, "Do not have other gods besides me" (Ex 20:3). In a dramatic display, Elijah confronted the prophets of Baal on Mount Carmel, and with fire from heaven showed the people that only God is worthy of our worship.

1KG 18:20–40

Self-Centered Worship

SIX

Our motive in worship should never be to impress others.

In the Sermon on the Mount, Jesus warned against acts of worship designed to make the worshiper look good to other people. In the book of Acts, we have the poor example of Ananias and Sapphira, who sold a property and gave a portion of the proceeds to the church in order to help those in need. They kept some of the money they received but lied in order to appear more generous than they really were. God's judgment was immediate.

MT 6:1, 5, 16; AC 5:1–11

Hypocritical Worship

SEVEN

Worship is an act of our hearts and our hands.

In the Old Testament, God rebuked His people for honoring Him with their lips but living lives that were anything but worshipful. They offered sacrifices and performed acts of technical obedience, but their hearts were far from Him (Is 29:13). Jesus echoed this same criticism to many of the religious leaders He encountered (Mt 15:7–9). True worship consists of offering God everything we have and everything we are.

LK 10:27; RM 12:1

Worship Apart from Spirit or Truth

EIGHT

God desires worship based on truth from a sincere heart.

Worship is no longer confined to a special location, like the temple that stood in Jerusalem long ago. Instead, as God's people, we have access to the Father, wherever we are, through His Spirit. Our worship should always be rooted in the truth of God's Word. As Jesus said, "An hour is coming, and is now here, when the true worshipers will worship the Father in Spirit and in truth" (Jn 4:23).

JN 4:1–26

THANKFULNESS IS CENTRAL TO A POSTURE OF WORSHIP.

Worship Through Gratitude

1 Chronicles 16:4–36
Ezra 3:10–11
Psalm 136

1 CHRONICLES 16:4-36

⁴ David appointed some of the Levites to be ministers before the ark of the Lᴏʀᴅ, to celebrate the Lᴏʀᴅ God of Israel, and to give thanks and praise to him. ⁵ Asaph was the chief and Zechariah was second to him. Jeiel, Shemiramoth, Jehiel, Mattithiah, Eliab, Benaiah, Obed-edom, and Jeiel played the harps and lyres, while Asaph sounded the cymbals ⁶ and the priests Benaiah and Jahaziel blew the trumpets regularly before the ark of the covenant of God.

DAVID'S PSALM OF THANKSGIVING

⁷ On that day David decreed for the first time that thanks be given to the Lᴏʀᴅ by Asaph and his relatives:

⁸ Give thanks to the Lᴏʀᴅ; call on his name;
proclaim his deeds among the peoples.
⁹ Sing to him; sing praise to him;
tell about all his wondrous works!
¹⁰ Honor his holy name;
let the hearts of those who seek the Lᴏʀᴅ rejoice.
¹¹ Seek the Lᴏʀᴅ and his strength;
seek his face always.
¹² Remember the wondrous works he has done,
his wonders, and the judgments he has pronounced,

Sing to him; sing praise to him; *tell about all his wondrous works!*

1 CHRONICLES 16:9

¹³ you offspring of Israel his servant,
Jacob's descendants—his chosen ones.

¹⁴ He is the Lord our God;
his judgments govern the whole earth.
¹⁵ Remember his covenant forever—
the promise he ordained for a thousand generations,
¹⁶ the covenant he made with Abraham,
swore to Isaac,
¹⁷ and confirmed to Jacob as a decree,
and to Israel as a permanent covenant:
¹⁸ "I will give the land of Canaan to you
as your inherited portion."

¹⁹ When they were few in number,
very few indeed, and resident aliens in Canaan
²⁰ wandering from nation to nation
and from one kingdom to another,
²¹ he allowed no one to oppress them;
he rebuked kings on their behalf:
²² "Do not touch my anointed ones
or harm my prophets."

²³ Let the whole earth sing to the Lord.
Proclaim his salvation from day to day.
²⁴ Declare his glory among the nations,
his wondrous works among all peoples.

²⁵ For the Lord is great and highly praised;
he is feared above all gods.
²⁶ For all the gods of the peoples are idols,
but the Lord made the heavens.
²⁷ Splendor and majesty are before him;
strength and joy are in his place.
²⁸ Ascribe to the Lord, families of the peoples,
ascribe to the Lord glory and strength.
²⁹ Ascribe to the Lord the glory of his name;
bring an offering and come before him.
Worship the Lord in the splendor of his holiness;
³⁰ let the whole earth tremble before him.
The world is firmly established;
it cannot be shaken.
³¹ Let the heavens be glad and the earth rejoice,
and let them say among the nations, "The Lord reigns!"
³² Let the sea and all that fills it resound;
let the fields and everything in them exult.

³³ Then the trees of the forest will shout for joy before
the LORD,
for he is coming to judge the earth.

³⁴ Give thanks to the LORD, for he is good;
his faithful love endures forever.
³⁵ And say: "Save us, God of our salvation;
gather us and rescue us from the nations
so that we may give thanks to your holy name
and rejoice in your praise.
³⁶ Blessed be the LORD God of Israel
from everlasting to everlasting."

Then all the people said, "Amen" and "Praise the LORD."

EZRA 3:10-11

TEMPLE FOUNDATION COMPLETED

¹⁰ When the builders had laid the foundation of the LORD's temple, the priests, dressed in their robes and holding trumpets, and the Levites descended from Asaph, holding cymbals, took their positions to praise the LORD, as King David of Israel had instructed. ¹¹ They sang with praise and thanksgiving to the LORD: "For he is good; his faithful love to Israel endures forever." Then all the people gave a great shout of praise to the LORD because the foundation of the LORD's house had been laid.

PSALM 136

GOD'S LOVE IS ETERNAL

¹ Give thanks to the LORD, for he is good.
His faithful love endures forever.
² Give thanks to the God of gods.
His faithful love endures forever.
³ Give thanks to the Lord of lords.
His faithful love endures forever.
⁴ He alone does great wonders.
His faithful love endures forever.
⁵ He made the heavens skillfully.
His faithful love endures forever.
⁶ He spread the land on the waters.
His faithful love endures forever.

⁷ He made the great lights:
His faithful love endures forever.
⁸ the sun to rule by day,
His faithful love endures forever.
⁹ the moon and stars to rule by night.
His faithful love endures forever.
¹⁰ He struck the firstborn of the Egyptians
His faithful love endures forever.
¹¹ and brought Israel out from among them
His faithful love endures forever.
¹² with a strong hand and outstretched arm.
His faithful love endures forever.
¹³ He divided the Red Sea
His faithful love endures forever.
¹⁴ and led Israel through,
His faithful love endures forever.
¹⁵ but hurled Pharaoh and his army into the Red Sea.
His faithful love endures forever.
¹⁶ He led his people in the wilderness.
His faithful love endures forever.
¹⁷ He struck down great kings
His faithful love endures forever.
¹⁸ and slaughtered famous kings—
His faithful love endures forever.
¹⁹ Sihon king of the Amorites
His faithful love endures forever.
²⁰ and Og king of Bashan—
His faithful love endures forever.
²¹ and gave their land as an inheritance,
His faithful love endures forever.
²² an inheritance to Israel his servant.
His faithful love endures forever.
²³ He remembered us in our humiliation
His faithful love endures forever.
²⁴ and rescued us from our foes.
His faithful love endures forever.
²⁵ He gives food to every creature.
His faithful love endures forever.
²⁶ Give thanks to the God of heaven!
His faithful love endures forever.

Reflect  Pray

DAY 5

WORSHIP THROUGH GRATITUDE

What do these scriptures say about worship through gratitude?

What does gratitude look like in this season of your life?

AS FOR ME AND MY FAMILY,
WE WILL WORSHIP THE LORD.

Use today to pray, rest, and reflect on
this week's reading, giving thanks for
the grace that is ours in Christ.

But if it doesn't please you to
worship the LORD, choose for
yourselves today: Which will
you worship—the gods your
fathers worshiped beyond the
Euphrates River or the gods
of the Amorites in whose land
you are living? As for me and
my family, we will worship
the LORD.

JOSHUA 24:15

Weekly Truth

Scripture is God-breathed and true. When we memorize it, we carry the gospel with us wherever we go.

This week we will memorize the key verse for this reading plan.

"But an hour is coming, and is now here, when the true worshipers will worship the Father in Spirit and in truth. *Yes, the Father wants such people to worship him.*"

JOHN 4:23

FIND THE CORRESPONDING <mark>MEMORY CARD</mark> IN THE BACK OF THIS BOOK.

WHEN WE SET OURSELVES APART FOR GOD, OUR LIVES CAN BECOME WORSHIP.

Worship Through Holiness

Leviticus 20:7–8
Isaiah 1:11–20
1 Peter 2:1–10
James 1:19–27

LEVITICUS 20:7-8

7 "Consecrate yourselves and be holy, for I am the LORD your God. 8 Keep my statutes and do them; I am the LORD who sets you apart."

ISAIAH 1:11-20

11 "What are all your sacrifices to me?"
asks the LORD.
"I have had enough of burnt offerings and rams
and the fat of well-fed cattle;
I have no desire for the blood of bulls,
lambs, or male goats.
12 When you come to appear before me,
who requires this from you—
this trampling of my courts?
13 Stop bringing useless offerings.
Your incense is detestable to me.
New Moons and Sabbaths,
and the calling of solemn assemblies—
I cannot stand iniquity with a festival.
14 I hate your New Moons and prescribed festivals.
They have become a burden to me;
I am tired of putting up with them.

"Consecrate yourselves and be holy, for I am the LORD your God."

LEVITICUS 20:7

15 When you spread out your hands in prayer,
I will refuse to look at you;
even if you offer countless prayers,
I will not listen.
Your hands are covered with blood.

PURIFICATION OF JERUSALEM

16 "Wash yourselves. Cleanse yourselves.
Remove your evil deeds from my sight.
Stop doing evil.
17 Learn to do what is good.
Pursue justice.
Correct the oppressor.
Defend the rights of the fatherless.
Plead the widow's cause.

18 "Come, let us settle this,"
says the LORD.
"Though your sins are scarlet,
they will be as white as snow;
though they are crimson red,
they will be like wool.

19 If you are willing and obedient,
you will eat the good things of the land.
20 But if you refuse and rebel,
you will be devoured by the sword."
For the mouth of the LORD has spoken.

1 PETER 2:1-10

THE LIVING STONE AND A HOLY PEOPLE

1 Therefore, rid yourselves of all malice, all deceit, hypocrisy, envy, and all slander. 2 Like newborn infants, desire the pure milk of the word, so that you may grow up into your salvation, 3 if you have tasted that the Lord is good. 4 As you come to him, a living stone—rejected by people but chosen and honored by God— 5 you yourselves, as living stones, a spiritual house, are being built to be a holy priesthood to offer spiritual sacrifices acceptable to God through Jesus Christ. 6 For it stands in Scripture:

See, I lay a stone in Zion,
a chosen and honored cornerstone,
and the one who believes in him
will never be put to shame.

7 So honor will come to you who believe; but for the unbelieving,

> The stone that the builders rejected—
> this one has become the cornerstone,

8 and

> A stone to stumble over,
> and a rock to trip over.

They stumble because they disobey the word; they were destined for this.

9 But you are a chosen race, a royal priesthood, a holy nation, a people for his possession, so that you may proclaim the praises of the one who called you out of darkness into his marvelous light. 10 Once you were not a people, but now you are God's people; you had not received mercy, but now you have received mercy.

JAMES 1:19-27

HEARING AND DOING THE WORD

19 My dear brothers and sisters, understand this: Everyone should be quick to listen, slow to speak, and slow to anger, 20 for human anger does not accomplish God's righteousness. 21 Therefore, ridding yourselves of all moral filth and the evil that is so prevalent, humbly receive the implanted word, which is able to save your souls.

22 But be doers of the word and not hearers only, deceiving yourselves. 23 Because if anyone is a hearer of the word and not a doer, he is like someone looking at his own face in a mirror. 24 For he looks at himself, goes away, and immediately forgets what kind of person he was. 25 But the one who looks intently into the perfect law of freedom and perseveres in it, and is not a forgetful hearer but a doer who works—this person will be blessed in what he does.

26 If anyone thinks he is religious without controlling his tongue, his religion is useless and he deceives himself. 27 Pure and undefiled religion before God the Father is this: to look after orphans and widows in their distress and to keep oneself unstained from the world.

Reflect & Pray

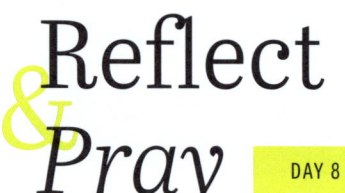

DAY 8

What do these scriptures say about worship through holiness?

What does pursuing holiness look like in this season of your life?

WHEN WE PRAY, WE WORSHIP GOD BY ALIGNING OUR WILL WITH HIS.

Worship Through Prayer

Matthew 6:5–15
Philippians 4:6–7
Psalm 44

MATTHEW 6:5-15

HOW TO PRAY

5 "Whenever you pray, you must not be like the hypocrites, because they love to pray standing in the synagogues and on the street corners to be seen by people. Truly I tell you, they have their reward. 6 But when you pray, go into your private room, shut your door, and pray to your Father who is in secret. And your Father who sees in secret will reward you. 7 When you pray, don't babble like the Gentiles, since they imagine they'll be heard for their many words. 8 Don't be like them, because your Father knows the things you need before you ask him.

THE LORD'S PRAYER

9 "Therefore, you should pray like this:

Our Father in heaven,
your name be honored as holy.
10 Your kingdom come.
Your will be done
on earth as it is in heaven.
11 Give us today our daily bread.
12 And forgive us our debts,
as we also have forgiven our debtors.
13 And do not bring us into temptation,
but deliver us from the evil one.

> "But when you pray, go into your private room, shut your door, and pray to your Father who is in secret. *And your Father who sees in secret will reward you.*"

MATTHEW 6:6

[14] "For if you forgive others their offenses, your heavenly Father will forgive you as well. [15] But if you don't forgive others, your Father will not forgive your offenses."

PHILIPPIANS 4:6–7

[6] Don't worry about anything, but in everything, through prayer and petition with thanksgiving, present your requests to God. [7] And the peace of God, which surpasses all understanding, will guard your hearts and minds in Christ Jesus.

PSALM 44

ISRAEL'S COMPLAINT

For the choir director. A Maskil of the sons of Korah.

[1] God, we have heard with our ears—
our ancestors have told us—
the work you accomplished in their days,
in days long ago:

[2] In order to plant them,
you displaced the nations by your hand;
in order to settle them,
you brought disaster on the peoples.
[3] For they did not take the land by their sword—
their arm did not bring them victory—
but by your right hand, your arm,
and the light of your face,
because you were favorable toward them.

[4] You are my King, my God,
who ordains victories for Jacob.
[5] Through you we drive back our foes;
through your name we trample our enemies.
[6] For I do not trust in my bow,
and my sword does not bring me victory.
[7] But you give us victory over our foes
and let those who hate us be disgraced.
[8] We boast in God all day long;
we will praise your name forever. *Selah*

⁹ But you have rejected and humiliated us;
you do not march out with our armies.
¹⁰ You make us retreat from the foe,
and those who hate us
have taken plunder for themselves.
¹¹ You hand us over to be eaten like sheep
and scatter us among the nations.
¹² You sell your people for nothing;
you make no profit from selling them.
¹³ You make us an object of reproach to our neighbors,
a source of mockery and ridicule to those around us.
¹⁴ You make us a joke among the nations,
a laughingstock among the peoples.
¹⁵ My disgrace is before me all day long,
and shame has covered my face,
¹⁶ because of the taunts of the scorner and reviler,
because of the enemy and avenger.

¹⁷ All this has happened to us,
but we have not forgotten you
or betrayed your covenant.
¹⁸ Our hearts have not turned back;
our steps have not strayed from your path.
¹⁹ But you have crushed us in a haunt of jackals
and have covered us with deepest darkness.
²⁰ If we had forgotten the name of our God
and spread out our hands to a foreign god,
²¹ wouldn't God have found this out,
since he knows the secrets of the heart?
²² Because of you we are being put to death all day long;
we are counted as sheep to be slaughtered.

²³ Wake up, Lord! Why are you sleeping?
Get up! Don't reject us forever!
²⁴ Why do you hide
and forget our affliction and oppression?
²⁵ For we have sunk down to the dust;
our bodies cling to the ground.
²⁶ Rise up! Help us!
Redeem us because of your faithful love.

Reflect & Pray

DAY 9

What do these scriptures say about worship through prayer?

What does prayer look like in this season of your life?

BECAUSE OF GOD'S GOODNESS TO US IN CHRIST, WE ARE FREE TO BE PEOPLE OF CELEBRATION.

Worship Through Celebration

Exodus 23:14–17
2 Samuel 6
Acts 2:46–47
Revelation 19:6–9
1 Corinthians 10:31

EXODUS 23:14-17

[14] "Celebrate a festival in my honor three times a year. [15] Observe the Festival of Unleavened Bread. As I commanded you, you are to eat unleavened bread for seven days at the appointed time in the month of Abib, because you came out of Egypt in that month. No one is to appear before me empty-handed. [16] Also observe the Festival of Harvest with the firstfruits of your produce from what you sow in the field, and observe the Festival of Ingathering at the end of the year, when you gather your produce from the field. [17] Three times a year all your males are to appear before the Lord GOD."

2 SAMUEL 6

DAVID MOVES THE ARK

[1] David again assembled all the fit young men in Israel: thirty thousand. [2] He and all his troops set out to bring the ark of God from Baale-judah. The ark bears the Name, the name of the LORD of Armies who is enthroned between the cherubim. [3] They set the ark of God on a new cart and transported it from Abinadab's house, which was on the hill. Uzzah and Ahio, sons of Abinadab, were guiding the cart [4] and brought it with the ark of God from Abinadab's house on the hill. Ahio walked in front of the ark. [5] David and the

I will dance before the LORD,
and I will dishonor myself and
humble myself even more.

2 SAMUEL 6:21-22

whole house of Israel were dancing before the LORD with all kinds of fir wood instruments, lyres, harps, tambourines, sistrums, and cymbals.

⁶ When they came to Nacon's threshing floor, Uzzah reached out to the ark of God and took hold of it because the oxen had stumbled. ⁷ Then the LORD's anger burned against Uzzah, and God struck him dead on the spot for his irreverence, and he died there next to the ark of God. ⁸ David was angry because of the LORD's outburst against Uzzah, so he named that place Outburst Against Uzzah, as it is today. ⁹ David feared the LORD that day and said, "How can the ark of the LORD ever come to me?" ¹⁰ So he was not willing to bring the ark of the LORD to the city of David; instead, he diverted it to the house of Obed-edom of Gath. ¹¹ The ark of the LORD remained in his house three months, and the LORD blessed Obed-edom and his whole family.

¹² It was reported to King David: "The LORD has blessed Obed-edom's family and all that belongs to him because of the ark of God." So David went and had the ark of God brought up from Obed-edom's house to the city of David with rejoicing. ¹³ When those carrying the ark of the LORD advanced six steps, he sacrificed an ox and a fattened calf.

¹⁴ David was dancing with all his might before the LORD wearing a linen ephod. ¹⁵ He and the whole house of Israel were bringing up the ark of the LORD with shouts and the sound of the ram's horn. ¹⁶ As the ark of the LORD was entering the city of David, Saul's daughter Michal looked down from the window and saw King David leaping and dancing before the LORD, and she despised him in her heart.

¹⁷ They brought the ark of the LORD and set it in its place inside the tent David had pitched for it. Then David offered burnt offerings and fellowship offerings in the LORD's presence. ¹⁸ When David had finished offering the burnt offering and the fellowship offerings, he blessed the people in the name of the LORD of Armies. ¹⁹ Then he distributed a loaf of bread, a date cake, and a raisin cake to each one in the entire Israelite community, both men and women. Then all the people went home.

²⁰ When David returned home to bless his household, Saul's daughter Michal came out to meet him. "How the king of Israel honored himself today!" she said. "He exposed himself today in the sight of the slave girls of his subjects like a vulgar person would expose himself."

²¹ David replied to Michal, "It was before the LORD who chose me over your father and his whole family to appoint me ruler over the LORD's people Israel. I will dance before the LORD, ²² and I will dishonor myself and humble myself even more. However, by the slave girls you spoke about, I will be honored." ²³ And Saul's daughter Michal had no child to the day of her death.

ACTS 2:46-47

⁴⁶ Every day they devoted themselves to meeting together in the temple, and broke bread from house to house. They ate their food with joyful and sincere hearts, ⁴⁷ praising God and enjoying the favor of all the people. Every day the Lord added to their number those who were being saved.

REVELATION 19:6-9

⁶ Then I heard something like the voice of a vast multitude, like the sound of cascading waters, and like the rumbling of loud thunder, saying,

Hallelujah, because our Lord God, the Almighty, reigns!
⁷ Let us be glad, rejoice, and give him glory, because the marriage of the Lamb has come, and his bride has prepared herself.
⁸ She was given fine linen to wear, bright and pure.

For the fine linen represents the righteous acts of the saints.

⁹ Then he said to me, "Write: Blessed are those invited to the marriage feast of the Lamb!" He also said to me, "These words of God are true."

1 CORINTHIANS 10:31

So, whether you eat or drink, or whatever you do, do everything for the glory of God.

Reflect & Pray

DAY 10

What do these scriptures say about worship through celebration?

What does celebration look like in this season of your life?

What Does the Bible Say About *Corporate Worship?*

Scripture calls us to worship God with other believers. However worship looks across our different denominations and traditions, when we gather together as the Church, we come to worship God and remember what He has done.

HERE IS A LOOK AT SOME OF WHAT THE BIBLE SAYS ABOUT WORSHIP IN COMMUNITY.

1

Corporate Worship in the *Old Testament*

Qahal is the Hebrew word often used for "assembly" in the Old Testament, referring to a group of people coming together for a particular purpose, typically worship or war.

JOS 18:1; 1KG 8:1-2; 2CH 20:26

God instructed the Israelites to gather together to remember how God brought them out of Egypt and to thank Him for all He had done.

LV 23

God's people came together in worship to dedicate themselves to the Lord and to their covenant with Him.

DT 29:1-32:47; 2KG 23:1-3; NEH 8-10

2

Corporate Worship in the *New Testament*

Ekklesia is the word used for *qahal* in the Greek translation of the Old Testament (known as the Septuagint). It was later used in the New Testament to describe both the Church in the universal sense and the church within a specific region.

AC 5:11; 8:1; 9:31; RM 16:5; RV 1:4

While teaching His disciples how to confront a sinful brother, Jesus promised that when two or three gather in His name, He will be there with them.

MT 18:20

The New Testament includes letters to different churches, encouraging them to continue gathering together and reminding them of their identity as God's people. Corporate worship in the early Church typically took place in people's homes and involved singing, teaching, eating together, participating in the Lord's Supper, praying for one another, and responding to the needs of the community.

AC 2:42-45; RM 16:23; 1CO 11:23-26; 14:26; JMS 5:16

3

Corporate Worship and *Believers*

Scripture includes many metaphors to describe the Church. These metaphors help believers understand their role in the world and the importance of gathering together.

- The Body of Christ
  1CO 12:20, 27; EPH 4:12; COL 1:18

- The Family of God
  MT 12:49-50; RM 8:16-17; 2CO 6:18; GL 6:10; 1JN 3:1

- The People of God
  PHP 3:20; 1PT 2:9; RV 1:6; RV 21:3

- The Temple of the Spirit
  1CO 3:16-17; 2CO 6:16; EPH 2:22

- The Bride of Christ
  2CO 11:2; EPH 5:22-33; RV 19:7

SACRIFICE IS AN INTIMATE ACT OF WORSHIP IN WHICH WE OFFER UP SOMETHING OF OURSELVES AND DRAW NEAR TO GOD.

Worship Through Sacrifice

Romans 12:1–2
Psalm 51
Luke 7:36–50
Hebrews 13:15–16

ROMANS 12:1-2

A LIVING SACRIFICE

[1] Therefore, brothers and sisters, in view of the mercies of God, I urge you to present your bodies as a living sacrifice, holy and pleasing to God; this is your true worship. [2] Do not be conformed to this age, but be transformed by the renewing of your mind, so that you may discern what is the good, pleasing, and perfect will of God.

PSALM 51

A PRAYER FOR RESTORATION

For the choir director. A psalm of David, when the prophet Nathan came to him after he had gone to Bathsheba.

[1] Be gracious to me, God,
according to your faithful love;
according to your abundant compassion,
blot out my rebellion.
[2] Completely wash away my guilt
and cleanse me from my sin.
[3] For I am conscious of my rebellion,
and my sin is always before me.

> # The sacrifice pleasing to God is a broken spirit. *You will not despise a broken and humbled heart, God.*
>
> PSALM 51:17

⁴ Against you—you alone—I have sinned
and done this evil in your sight.
So you are right when you pass sentence;
you are blameless when you judge.
⁵ Indeed, I was guilty when I was born;
I was sinful when my mother conceived me.

⁶ Surely you desire integrity in the inner self,
and you teach me wisdom deep within.
⁷ Purify me with hyssop, and I will be clean;
wash me, and I will be whiter than snow.
⁸ Let me hear joy and gladness;
let the bones you have crushed rejoice.
⁹ Turn your face away from my sins
and blot out all my guilt.

¹⁰ God, create a clean heart for me
and renew a steadfast spirit within me.
¹¹ Do not banish me from your presence
or take your Holy Spirit from me.
¹² Restore the joy of your salvation to me,
and sustain me by giving me a willing spirit.
¹³ Then I will teach the rebellious your ways,
and sinners will return to you.

¹⁴ Save me from the guilt of bloodshed, God —
God of my salvation—
and my tongue will sing of your righteousness.
¹⁵ Lord, open my lips,
and my mouth will declare your praise.
¹⁶ You do not want a sacrifice, or I would give it;
you are not pleased with a burnt offering.
¹⁷ The sacrifice pleasing to God is a broken spirit.
You will not despise a broken and humbled heart, God.

¹⁸ In your good pleasure, cause Zion to prosper;
build the walls of Jerusalem.
¹⁹ Then you will delight in righteous sacrifices,
whole burnt offerings;
then bulls will be offered on your altar.

LUKE 7:36-50

MUCH FORGIVENESS, MUCH LOVE

³⁶ Then one of the Pharisees invited him to eat with him. He entered the Pharisee's house and reclined at the table. ³⁷ And a woman in the town who was a sinner found out that Jesus was reclining at the table in the Pharisee's house.

She brought an alabaster jar of perfume [38] and stood behind him at his feet, weeping, and began to wash his feet with her tears. She wiped his feet with her hair, kissing them and anointing them with the perfume.

[39] When the Pharisee who had invited him saw this, he said to himself, "This man, if he were a prophet, would know who and what kind of woman this is who is touching him—she's a sinner!"

[40] Jesus replied to him, "Simon, I have something to say to you."

He said, "Say it, teacher."

[41] "A creditor had two debtors. One owed five hundred denarii, and the other fifty. [42] Since they could not pay it back, he graciously forgave them both. So, which of them will love him more?"

[43] Simon answered, "I suppose the one he forgave more."

"You have judged correctly," he told him. [44] Turning to the woman, he said to Simon, "Do you see this woman? I entered your house; you gave me no water for my feet, but she, with her tears, has washed my feet and wiped them with her hair. [45] You gave me no kiss, but she hasn't stopped kissing my feet since I came in. [46] You didn't anoint my head with olive oil, but she has anointed my feet with perfume. [47] Therefore I tell you, her many sins have been forgiven; that's why she loved much. But the one who is forgiven little, loves little." [48] Then he said to her, "Your sins are forgiven."

[49] Those who were at the table with him began to say among themselves, "Who is this man who even forgives sins?"

[50] And he said to the woman, "Your faith has saved you. Go in peace."

HEBREWS 13:15-16

[15] Therefore, through him let us continually offer up to God a sacrifice of praise, that is, the fruit of lips that confess his name. [16] Don't neglect to do what is good and to share, for God is pleased with such sacrifices.

Reflect & Pray

DAY 11

What do these scriptures say about worship through sacrifice?

What does sacrifice to God look like in this season of your life?

WE MAGNIFY GOD'S NAME WHEN WE TELL OTHERS ABOUT HIM.

Worship Through Proclamation

Deuteronomy 32:3–4
Nehemiah 8:1–12
John 9:13–38

DEUTERONOMY 32:3-4

³ For I will proclaim the Lord's name.
Declare the greatness of our God!
⁴ The Rock—his work is perfect;
all his ways are just.
A faithful God, without bias,
he is righteous and true.

NEHEMIAH 8:1-12

PUBLIC READING OF THE LAW

¹ When the seventh month came and the Israelites had settled in their towns, all the people gathered together at the square in front of the Water Gate. They asked the scribe Ezra to bring the book of the law of Moses that the Lord had given Israel. ² On the first day of the seventh month, the priest Ezra brought the law before the assembly of men, women, and all who could listen with understanding. ³ While he was facing the square in front of the Water Gate, he read out of it from daybreak until noon before the men, the women, and those who could understand. All the people listened attentively to the book of the law. ⁴ The scribe Ezra stood on a high wooden platform made for this purpose. Mattithiah, Shema, Anaiah, Uriah, Hilkiah, and Maaseiah stood beside him

For I will proclaim the LORD's name. *Declare the greatness of our God!*

DEUTERONOMY 32:3

on his right; to his left were Pedaiah, Mishael, Malchijah, Hashum, Hash-baddanah, Zechariah, and Meshullam. [5] Ezra opened the book in full view of all the people, since he was elevated above everyone. As he opened it, all the people stood up. [6] Ezra blessed the LORD, the great God, and with their hands uplifted all the people said, "Amen, Amen!" Then they knelt low and worshiped the LORD with their faces to the ground.

[7] Jeshua, Bani, Sherebiah, Jamin, Akkub, Shabbethai, Hodiah, Maaseiah, Kelita, Azariah, Jozabad, Hanan, and Pelaiah, who were Levites, explained the law to the people as they stood in their places. [8] They read out of the book of the law of God, translating and giving the meaning so that the people could understand what was read. [9] Nehemiah the governor, Ezra the priest and scribe, and the Levites who were instructing the people said to all of them, "This day is holy to the LORD your God. Do not mourn or weep." For all the people were weeping as they heard the words of the law. [10] Then he said to them, "Go and eat what is rich, drink what is sweet, and send portions to those who have nothing prepared, since today is holy to our Lord. Do not grieve, because the joy of the LORD is your strength." [11] And the Levites quieted all the people, saying, "Be still, since today is holy. Don't grieve." [12] Then all the people began to eat and drink, send portions, and have a great celebration, because they had understood the words that were explained to them.

JOHN 9:13-38

THE HEALED MAN'S TESTIMONY

[13] They brought the man who used to be blind to the Pharisees. [14] The day that Jesus made the mud and opened his eyes was a Sabbath. [15] Then the Pharisees asked him again how he received his sight.

"He put mud on my eyes," he told them. "I washed and I can see."

[16] Some of the Pharisees said, "This man is not from God, because he doesn't keep the Sabbath." But others were saying, "How can a sinful man perform such signs?" And there was a division among them.

[17] Again they asked the blind man, "What do you say about him, since he opened your eyes?"

"He's a prophet," he said.

[18] The Jews did not believe this about him—that he was blind and received sight—until they summoned the parents of the one who had received his sight.

[19] They asked them, "Is this your son, the one you say was born blind? How then does he now see?"

20 "We know this is our son and that he was born blind," his parents answered. 21 "But we don't know how he now sees, and we don't know who opened his eyes. Ask him; he's of age. He will speak for himself." 22 His parents said these things because they were afraid of the Jews, since the Jews had already agreed that if anyone confessed him as the Messiah, he would be banned from the synagogue. 23 This is why his parents said, "He's of age; ask him."

24 So a second time they summoned the man who had been blind and told him, "Give glory to God. We know that this man is a sinner."

25 He answered, "Whether or not he's a sinner, I don't know. One thing I do know: I was blind, and now I can see!"

26 Then they asked him, "What did he do to you? How did he open your eyes?"

27 "I already told you," he said, "and you didn't listen. Why do you want to hear it again? You don't want to become his disciples too, do you?"

28 They ridiculed him: "You're that man's disciple, but we're Moses's disciples. 29 We know that God has spoken to Moses. But this man—we don't know where he's from."

30 "This is an amazing thing!" the man told them. "You don't know where he is from, and yet he opened my eyes. 31 We know that God doesn't listen to sinners, but if anyone is God-fearing and does his will, he listens to him. 32 Throughout history no one has ever heard of someone opening the eyes of a person born blind. 33 If this man were not from God, he wouldn't be able to do anything."

34 "You were born entirely in sin," they replied, "and are you trying to teach us?" Then they threw him out.

SPIRITUAL BLINDNESS

35 Jesus heard that they had thrown the man out, and when he found him, he asked, "Do you believe in the Son of Man?"

36 "Who is he, Sir, that I may believe in him?" he asked.

37 Jesus answered, "You have seen him; in fact, he is the one speaking with you."

38 "I believe, Lord!" he said, and he worshiped him.

Reflect & Pray

DAY 12

What do these scriptures say about worship through proclamation?

What does proclamation look like in this season of your life?

DON'T NEGLECT TO DO WHAT IS GOOD
AND TO SHARE, FOR GOD IS PLEASED
WITH SUCH SACRIFICES.

Use today to pray, rest, and reflect on
this week's reading, giving thanks for
the grace that is ours in Christ.

Therefore, through him let us
continually offer up to God
a sacrifice of praise, that is,
the fruit of lips that confess
his name. Don't neglect to
do what is good and to share,
for God is pleased with such
sacrifices.

HEBREWS 13:15–16

Weekly Truth

Scripture is God-breathed and true. When we memorize it, we carry the gospel with us wherever we go.

This week we will memorize a call to worship God in our daily lives.

Therefore, brothers and sisters, in view of the mercies of God, I urge you to present your bodies as a living sacrifice, holy and pleasing to God; *this is your true worship.*

ROMANS 12:1

FIND THE CORRESPONDING MEMORY CARD IN THE BACK OF THIS BOOK.

WORSHIP IS NOT AN EXPERIENCE. WORSHIP IS AN ACT, AND THIS TAKES DISCIPLINE. WE ARE TO WORSHIP

"IN SPIRIT AND IN TRUTH." NEVER MIND ABOUT THE FEELINGS. WE ARE TO WORSHIP IN SPITE OF THEM.

ELISABETH ELLIOT

DOWNLOAD THE APP

STOP BY
shereadstruth.com

SHOP
shopshereadstruth.com

SEND A NOTE
hello@shereadstruth.com

SHARE
#SheReadsTruth

BIBLIOGRAPHY

Derek Leigh Davis, "Assembly, Religious," ed. Douglas Mangum et al., *Lexham Theological Wordbook,* Lexham Bible Reference Series. Bellingham, WA: Lexham Press, 2014.

Harrison, John, ed. and James D. Dvorak, ed. *The New Testament Church: The Challenge of Developing Ecclesiologies.* Eugene, OR: Pickwick Publications, 2012.

SHE READS TRUTH *is a worldwide community of women who read God's Word together every day.*

Founded in 2012, She Reads Truth invites women of all ages to engage with Scripture through daily reading plans, online conversation led by a vibrant community of contributors, and offline resources created at the intersection of beauty, goodness, and Truth.

e Day

rest and reflect on this week's reading,
grace that is ours in Christ.

Yours, LORD, is the
greatness and the
power and the glory
and the splendor
and the majesty,
for everything in
the heavens and on
earth belongs to you.

Yours, LORD, is the kingdom, and you
are exalted as head over all. Riches
and honor come from you, and you
are the ruler of everything. Power and
might are in your hand, and it is in
your hand to make great and to give
strength to all. Now therefore, our
God, we give you thanks and praise
your glorious name.

1 CHRONICLES 29:11–13

If you enjoyed this study on biblical worship, we recommend **Give Thanks: A Study of Biblical Gratitude**.

True gratitude is a posture of worship. It is the habit of turning our hearts and minds to the active work of God. In this three-week reading plan, you'll learn what Scripture has to say about giving thanks in all seasons—in times of joy and sorrow, plenty and want, work and rest, and more.

WHERE DID I STUDY?

O HOME

O OFFICE

O COFFEE SHOP

O CHURCH

O A FRIEND'S HOUSE

O OTHER

WHAT WAS I LISTENING TO?

ARTIST:

SONG:

PLAYLIST:

WHEN DID I STUDY?

MORNING

AFTERNOON

NIGHT

What did I learn?

WHAT WAS HAPPENING IN MY LIFE?

WHAT WAS HAPPENING IN THE WORLD?

MONTH	DAY	YEAR

END DATE

"But an hour is coming, and is now here, when the true worshipers will worship the Father

in Spirit
& *in truth.*

Yes, the Father wants such people to worship him."

THEREFORE, BROTHERS AND SISTERS, IN VIEW OF THE MERCIES OF GOD, I URGE YOU TO PRESENT YOUR BODIES AS A LIVING SACRIFICE, HOLY AND PLEASING TO GOD; THIS IS YOUR TRUE WORSHIP.

Romans 12:1

DEUTERONOMY 32:3

For I will proclaim the LORD's name.
Declare the greatness of our God!

LET'S MEMORIZE GOD'S WORD TOGETHER.

These Scripture memory cards correspond to the Weekly Truths in the **In Spirit & in Truth: A Study of Biblical Worship** reading plan.

Punch out the cards and carry them with you, place them where you'll see them often, or share them with a friend.

Bonus Card!

SHE READS TRUTH

WOMEN IN THE WORD
OF GOD EVERY DAY

SHEREADSTRUTH.COM
hello@shereadstruth.com
@shereadstruth

SHE READS TRUTH

WOMEN IN THE WORD
OF GOD EVERY DAY

SHEREADSTRUTH.COM
hello@shereadstruth.com
@shereadstruth

SHE READS TRUTH

WOMEN IN THE WORD
OF GOD EVERY DAY

SHEREADSTRUTH.COM
hello@shereadstruth.com
@shereadstruth